WORDS OF
OUR LORD
JESUS CHRIST

TOMMIE LINDSEY

Book Vine Press
2516 Highland Dr.
Palatine, IL 60067

For why do you fall for Satan Deception

Why do you allow Satans lies to grow in your head for if you look closer you'll see it's just a illusion a made-up thought just to fool your spirit and everything that he tries to used on you in the first place is full of steroids just to make his lies to you look much bigger than what they are as Christians we are no fool when we use God's fuel which is the holy Bible for burning up the deceitful lies of the devil.

The Bible

The Bible says seek God with your whole heart but there are probably some Christians that goes to church with a cold heart not fully giving God the praise that he truly deserve and some may even go with a Luke warm heart knowing that there Spirit are confused and unsure about how a holy ghost feel Christians should be loving and kind to their neighbor as well Jesus was when he went to the cross for our sins and that is how Jesus showed us his love the end.

Cloning there is so...

There are some people with strong ambition that's say if I could clone myself three times I would be three times richer in then there are other peoples that don't want to work but just plain lazy that would say if I could clone myself three times I would just be three times still poorer

The NRA

The NRA they are not looking at the numbers of human life there guns take each year but the numbers of dollars that goes into there stockholders bank account each year that really is what's called blood money for each dollar that they receive really does have someone else's blood on it for all the politicians and gun makers just think for the heat that it taken to make that gun will not take away but will add to the heat in hell for your soul for the gun that you have created to take away another one of God's humans life in someone else's soul

The price of freedom

Freedom ain't free in the first place there was a great price for our sins and our father God pay it through the crucifixion which took place at the cross with his son Jesus who died for us and on the third day the Lord rose again so you now know that freedom ain't free because Jesus paid the price for you and for me-a shout out to all the military forces of the United States of America each individual that died for our freedom now thank again because freedom ain't free there was some military person that gave up his life for you and for me

Pure of heart

God say we must be pure of heart after all we are human and spiritual beings children's of the most high God at the same time Satan fights against our heart as he tries to place uncleanlyness in our sould as well throughout our life but thanks to Our Father God it won't be so

The Cycle

There was a time when the elderly paid us to lift boxes and some other heavy items and now that we also became elderly we also now paid the younger people to perform some of the same chores that the elderlies pay us for and other word that is a never-ending cycle and will not stop until we receive our Heavenly Body that we know will be presented to us in heaven

One out of two groups

Food for thought just think if you did a survey on two group of people one group you place them in the front of a tv for one month just watching the report on the Covid 19 and the other group didn't watch the news on TV that month but did just sit back and enjoy the reading of their Bible now out of the two groups of people whom do you think will find the most peace within themselves the one that serve our Lord God or the one that have set back and watch the TV new and now have found themself in a much more of a stressful situation. For this is Our God time or your over worked mine

Learn to honor God flock

To some of you pastor's whom don't seems to be taking our God will and words to Heart for you know that it's not the full obligation of the government to provide for the children's of God meaning that the church should be taking on more responsibility when it comes to dealing with the needs of the children of abab Father God not totally looking for the needs of the help from the government but facing up for we know where our joy and help, come from is the Lord our God

When God speaks

When God spoke this world into existence then he said that it is good then later he created man and it is good so we now thank that man can destroy something that God said that it's good God made all preparation for all of his creations so the world has a way of sustaining its boundary what you really need to be concentrating on is the need to bring the spirit of God back into a Lost generation

False prophet

Satan is called the prince of this world that may be right but one thing we know for sure that he will never become king so why would you keep on kneeling down following a prince that means you no good when you can embrace the true king the Messiah and in one day be able to gather at the table in the throne of God-All praises be to God

A world full of deception

There are some people that think for themselves but then there are some people that need others to help them take care of some other type of business in the meantime they are seriously being taken advantage of in one way or another again they are only thinking about themselves that shows you that in this selfish and unbelievable world that the full measure of greed will never leave but there will always be a lot of people waiting to be scammed or deceived. (Thank God for his goodness).

Problems and solutions

Like some people's problem that you are dealing with have truly become yours and then it feels like they have become part of your body seem like they are grabbing your blood vessel and squeezing them stopping your blood at times from making circulations to your heart therefore it seems like that it's missing a beat and when the grip is release then the fluttering of your heart seems to increase. Now some people's with headaches and some with back aches now put this together why because the circumstances have someone else's problems leaning on your body and mind hopefully the symptoms will not bother you physically or mentally in time. (Amen)

I praise God the Creator for giving me the opportunity to experience this thing call life for if God haven't picked up the dust from the ground and blowed life into it then we would have never known about a loving and holy God all praise to my father God.

Food for thought: Just think when Eve was having a conversation with the snake he was telling her everything she wanted to hear and then see begin to hear what she wanted to hear from the mouth of Satan those words was spoken like Venom which in true form is another word for poison that Eve took into here body.

Reunions

Have you every taken the time and thought about all the family reunions that you have attend and being thankful for seeing all your cousins that you have not seen like in Forever. So maybe you had a good time and enjoyed some of your cousin company. But at the same time haven't forgetting about the ones that we're dead and went to heaven. Therefore we all should strive for holiness in order to be saved that we all will make it into heaven. And there rejoicing in a real heavenly family reunions all praises to our God.

Your Phone

There used to be a time when people used to hold satan under their feet but nowdays they hold him in their hands and up to their ears so close that they won't have to strain to Here while taking bad thought into their mind and heart instead of rebuking Satan they listen to him as though he were saying something that they wanted to hear a suggestion that you take the phone away from your ear and place satan back under your feet amen

Blinded to Our God's door

Can you imagine some parents getting up on Sunday morning as they get their children ddressed just to accompany them to the liquor store as they passes up our God churches door

Stop deceiving yourself

You have some people walking on Gods Earth thinking that they are entitled to the things of others in life at no cost you need to rethink your situation because things in life are not free while you are going through life but at the same time going out backwards for our god did say that you would have to work and eat from the sweat of your very own brow meaning that there is no one whom will have to support your need as you sit back and waste your god giving seed which is your money on a disgusting habit that you really don't need so stop perpetrating and turn to God for he is the only one that can Supply your every need at the same time take away your very bad habit that some people's want to call a disease so don't despair or lose hope because God have has a cure for all of our needs by taking it to Christ Jesus At The Cross and leave it there. Praise God.

Your goodness return home

We know that Jesus returned to Glory and prepared your heavenly home which is your very own mansion so does the Good Deeds that you perform on Earth go before you to help prepare your mansion in heaven could it also means that the bad Deeds that you do also descendant back into the home that you have created in the pits of hell meaning that it could intense and super increase the fire that you have made in your very own portions of Hell which is your new home and your very own creation for not choosing to do the will of God. (all praises to our God)

Only Our God can judge and for any reason that we might want to (assume) we may be sinning and not knowing that we are also acting like the judge

In my God hand

God show me some years ago about something that was soon to take place with my son and that it would be physical enemy but everything that satan had an his artilery like the fiery Dart and so much more to harm my family but thanks to my God he had already placed his Heavenly armies of Angels exactly where he wanted them to be located and

I thank the Lord that he did show me in my dream where there was a stone angel in my backyard facing north and as I began to walk towards it began to turn South facing my house with a smile upon its face as though it was saying that your God have everything under control why because my God have everything in the palm of his hand in I thank God for that and had to pray and leave it there so now I know that the Lord was saying to me that I needed the shield of faith in order for everything to be made somewhat easier and return back to the sender Satan for I know my God has everything under control letting me know that the battle is not mine but the Lords I praise God that the Lord says what he means and of course means what he say and I know therefore that it could not had been left and a better place Our God hand

Eternity

Love everlasting you can take one drop of Jesus blood and create a unlimited number of universes and with that same drop you can overpopulate those same universes get the picture will just one drop of the Lamb blood thing does last forever therefore you know that eternity has no end so think before you allow yourself to sin becaue there is a place where you really don't care to an because the fire can't be quiet so you know there's no end it's like dose flames have always been there for those who refuse not too stop sining in hell you won't recognize your so-called friend because everyone will look the same as they burn in those unholy flames why won't people unpopulated hell and leave Satan there to be tormented in his own inconvenient cell

Take two guesses

Just thank here in America we have two Rich twins Brothers aguesses to who they are one like having his finger pointed at you in the other one like to threaten you and have his hands in your pockets again one guesses to who they are then if you guess Uncle Sam in the IRS you guessed correct

Last call before you fall

To all you young man and women who can bravely say I ain't scared of dying that could be true now figure this one out not about dying but when you open up your eyes then you have breathe your last dying breath that's what's going to come as the shocker. Because in hell young man you won't be able to stash or carry a glock (Which represent a)

GUN So you should make God your first call before you do your last fall (Amen)

Keep hope alive

We all face things in our lives but what makes it crazy when Satan comes and think that I'm going to just sit back and allow him to think that he's going to make my life sad, Satan I got just a few words for you to comprehend you may be a convincing liar but this is one child that will not buy into your fabrication, so I will kindly put my feet down and only God knows where they will land and that's right directly on the top of your head just to let you know that I am God's child and have always Been covered with his blood and refuse to give in.

Your truth

People walking around in this world saying now look what Satan made me do if you felt that way then for what no good reason would you listen to him ask though that the only voice, that you care to hear is that one wow being disobeident why don't you hear the voice of God maybe you really don't care, there for you just refuse to pay it any attention so then the only voice you care to hear is the one that means you know worldly good but you still Received it for your actual truth Amen

You have a line to God

You are just one call away from God and that call is his son Christ Jesus so just think if you was to pick up the phone and that line represent Christ Jesus So the line that you are talking on goes directly to God knowing that when you pray your call may get a answer right away be believing and having no doubt our God will surely work things out Praise God

Misuse

To all the ladies and men who want to play your mate for a sucker you can only play and lick on your sucker for so long and after that you know that the sucker is gone and you are left with a unhappy home all because you licked and eaten on and play that so-called sucker your're left with a bitter taste in your mouth in all alone.

Scapegoat

Someone to punish when you don't want the blame to fall on the real culprit which is yourself there will always be some scapegoat that wat truly stand up for themselves but take the blame for others that they think are their friends if they were they would not have allowed you to have taken the blame for misdeed in the first place not your friend BUT USER IN THE END

God's filling

I am feeling what I feel and it's not fear for God never gave us the power of fear but he did give us the power of love so with that to eloquently place in our spirit all we need is to continuously push forward as witnessess for the glory of God here on Earth to manifest what we need be for the kingdom of God (We know the meaning of The great I am) (God feeling what I feel and it's not fear)

Adultery

Adultery is when you cheat on God with someone else and now you and that someone else is cheating on your spose now how would you feel if you was married to that someone else and they were doing the same thing to you behind your back that wouldn't be a happy feeling because there's nothing good about adultery when you are breaking up someone else's home you know it takes two to tango so don't be obnoxious leave that other one alone because if not God will decide to destroy your sinful and adultery ways Praise God

What the Lord hands hold

The love of Jesus Christ you may feel that you'er ambition had dropped but in due time you will know that you have not because the lord Jesus Christ will not allows you to fall through his nail-scarred hands God have everything under control and therefore you should have no doubt because our God had already laid everything out the plans and blessings for your life and all you have to do is just follow them through as children of God

Students

Just think we're students of the Holy Spirit that desire to dwell within us and to teach us the ways of our God we will never fully understand but we must start somewhere in order for us to start comprehending the truth that awaits our spirits it's all about the will and wanting to learn to accomplish this class in order to start on the right Journey to God and to accomplish the guidance of the holy spirit that he have placed in US to make the journey much more manageable.

Bricks and mortar

To all of you pastors whom keep spending God's tithe on brick and mortar when it should only be used to locate lost souls and not contine being wasted on building that will matter in the end will be the one that awaits us in heaven that the Lord have designed for his children in heaven which is you're very only mention so now is the time that the mismange of God fund be put to good use like putting Satan on his guard and on the run

Judgement day

We should be bowing Down On Our Knees each and every day giving our God praise for accepting and allowing his only son the right to receive the sin and weight of this entire deceitful and sinful world into his body but yet even today this very world still refuse to show our God love and gratitude for what Jesus did on the cross for The People this will certainly not have been done invain but most definitely The Sinner will be put to shame for the one that does not repent and show remorse for there sinning against our Holy father for it seems like the more people try to change the more sin try to step into play the most un Holiness of games plus it seems as though sine have grown so rapidly and these last days and so outrageous today in for that you know each and every sinner have already now been asigned a Doomsday in which they will have to pay in the lake of fire on Judgement Day

Agape love

Christians have chosen to serve God while the unsaved ones live out there lives acting like heathens living with attitudes instead of with Grace for what our God has allowed Jesus to show commitment and the true Act Of love At The Cross on the behalf of God's children's so therefore we should be praising our God through the life and time of his only son Christ Jesus while taking into our body the Holy Spirit through the death and Resurrection from the shedding of the blood from our Lord Jesus while acknowledging the love of God and also to perform that same type of love that our God showed to us by passing out to others the same type of agape love that God has given to us his children. (Praise God)

Satan's lies

How many of us have ever wonder about the snake being a beast in the field and that before he tempted Eve in the garden that he might have had legs protruding out of it's body but due to the rebellious thought that he placed into the mind of Eve God has taken away his legs and now his belly has became his leg and feet making him now one of the most lowest crawling Beast of God's creation some people are like snake but hoping that they don't spit out poisonous venom or lies but have learned how to tell the god honest whole truth in order to rebuke the lies of Satan. Amen

Listening ears

A reminder to all the people even though we were not there over 2000 years ago there was a pass over that did occur and God's children were told to place the blood of a lamb on there doorpost for their protection from death and now over 2000 years later the angel of death have passed again not to free God's people from Egypt but from there sin woo to God's people who have listening ears but still refuse to hear. Will your spirit be full of God's grace or will you allow fear to take it's please

The sword

Say for instance if our God would have placed steel inside man's heart for we know that God's words are as a two-edged sword made of holy steel which respresent the words of God's sometimes we allow our steel to be unsharpended by the lies of Satan so then it needs to be resharpended. Thought Jesus blood in the words of God so that we may return and continue to fight the ways and the sins of the devil

Take away the consent

We give the devil too much praise when it comes to being smart truly all that it is as Christians we have a tendency of letting down our guard so now that we know the truth we need to repent and take away the consent for allowing Satan to think that he can manipulate our hearts so now we need to take away his so-called smart just to let him know that he doesn't control Christians hearts or any part of their soul

Never ending

Some people look down the neck of a bottle of alcohol hoping that the bottom never goes dry and others look down the neck of a drug pipe hoping that the base of the pipe never goes empty others roll marijuana joints hoping that the paper that they're roll it in would last a lifetime some look down the eye of a drug needles into a spoon or any other type of container that they may use as they used there drug in abused their body some really do have excruciating pain and that is when they really should be calling on the name of our Lord and savior there are some that have pain that is truly made up in their brains and some of them uses just to make themselves feel good but through it all they all are making the wrong call bye bringing on themselves the Spirit of death that they may not be able too back off so before you lose your soul look up and behold and call on the name of the Lord. Amen

Information on prideful

Information about a prideful person when a son can't talk to his dad or a daughter to her mother about something that's going on within themselves I feel that their pain increase you know God is not content with a prideful person that won't allow our Father God to help them so they continued suffering and hurt more then others inside why because they want push that foolish pride to the side for God can help them in order for them to survive

Peace from God

As Christian we should be saying I am too blessed in order to be stress therefore I feel my soul and spirit is at rest while leaning on the piece from our God for I know that he is where my peace come from for after all God is The great I am and that makes us at peace with our God

Taking God out of the school

They have taken our God out of the school and now the devil makes the rule they have taken the Bible out of school and now guns are what they use we shold be turning against some schools just to let them know that the devil doesn't make the rules

Peace was granite

Just a few words to take into your heart please don't wait til this world begin to burn before you learn to call on the name of Jesus so many of you call on God our Father why you keep on refusing and neglecting to give acknowledgement to his only son Christ Jesus in his proper seat at the right hand of his father so when will you stop rejecting him and give Jesus Christ his property do because the longer you wait the more you also stand to lose so why not give in to Jesus like he gave it all in at the cross for you by remembering that beore he return back to our Father God he left us all with some commandments you should go out to all four corners of the Earth and make believers out of all those peoples that have no faith about what Jesus did at the cross for us all in order that we will have eternal life in joining him and our Earth family at the right hand of Our Father God in Paradise and then you can truly say that there is no place like our Heavenly home

Weakest link

Some people want to call Eve weak and that maybe right after all she May have came from the weakest part of Adam's Rib that means Adam could have been much more of a man because we are only as strong as our weakest link.

Calling for your life

I sincerely feel that we should have a spiritual talk with God and ask him to remove the scales of doubt from our eyes that we may see our true calling from Heaven in respond to the calling that God has placed in our life for his glory.

God love

I praise God the Creator for giving me the opportunity to experience this thing call life for if God haven't picked up the dust from the ground and blowed life into it then we would have never known about a loving and holy God all praise to my father God.

Pure heart

God said we must be pure of heart after all we are human and Children of the most high God and at the same time Satan's fights against our hearts as he tried to place uncleanness within our spirit that conflict with the words of Abba Father God

Hold unto the rock of God

God is our Rock and salvation instead of picking up the Rock which is God's good word and placing it in to our heart some have the nerves to toss the work of God to the ground and then begin kicking it around therefore some have truly have missed out on the true love of God.

True colors

There are lots of friendly politicians that lied their way into office and once they are there it's time for their true colors to come out why because they are not your true leader so then problems arise then it's time to pick a side and now they begin stepping on the back of the poor just to convince the other side.

A child gift

Children like getting present for birthday and Christmas as they grow up and become adults hoping that they would rejoice and receive the most wonderful present of all and that is the presence of the most high God in our life.

There are

There are some pastors who is treating God ministry as a business by building these big aesthetics builders to glorify themselves instead of feeding the poor the widow in the offenset just think when Jesus returns will he knocked over those buildings as he did the tax collectors tables for worshiping the buildings and not our Lord Jesus Christ

We were made in the image of God but as some grow up it's like some of their Gods genes have lost it's way into their hearts as well their will to accept Gods love so therefore a long the way some have aloud Satan DNA to join into their soul to play and now sin has set in so now those people have lost their way and for that they must pay for refusing to accept God Gene and now hell is how they will pay.

The land of Israel

We know that Israel is the apple of God eyes and also his chosen peoples which is the Israelites and everything that is not spiritually clean want to take a chunk out of the city that is forbidden that our God calls his very own now think back into the garden of Eden which is Our God's also again we were told not to take a bite from the fruit of the Forbidden tree and again God words was not obey or even heard why becaue now they want to take a even bigger portion out of the land of Israel which we know is our God Prime Property and possession Israel and we know that in the first place it's should not have been thought about or even touched in anyway but again Satan had to try and have his own way and again Satan was rejected because therewill be no way that God will allow Satan to have the last saying now lets Adventure even further back when before the so-called angel of Light became a enemy of Our Father God because he wanted to try and overtake the kingdom of heaven from a

Choose Wisely

Have you chosen your place for eternal life or are you now just waiting to see the outcome by you not deciding to choose Jesus you can say it's have already been made a choice and not a very smart one have you ever received a third degree burn they are very painful but in hell they don't compare so what you need to do is lay your Sin at the foot of the cross because there are no other place in between heaven or hell is the last scene

God reach

You can take the fullness of the entire universe and fit it in our God holy hand it's would not even represent or bethe half of a side of a whole grain of sand and other words there is nothing that our mind can be hold or comprehend about our God in his expansion in other words there is nothing that out of the reach of Our Lord God so therefore his love last and reaches out into alleternity where we know that there is no end

Not so good choice

Think about this why does some people knowingly or unnowingly allow other people the right to dictate where they will spend eternity when they should actually be bowing down on their knees and praying before our God instead your allowing some person that's in your life whom wont commit to you through marriage or who wont even truly help them to Carrie or even bear there burden but they do give them the right to make a final decision for them that have you laying on a Unholy made-up bed which represent fornification which will leave you right into the fiery pits of hell which is not where you want to reside or even lay there for one day so just think about laying there burning each and every moment aout a choice that could have made differently when it came to living and serving the lord

It's been a

It's been said before if we wanted to the ladies could rule the world just think when God created Eve he did not say Eve name the animals or when Eve fell asleep God didn't decide to take a rib from Eve to create Adam as her mate but the other way around also it was not Adam that took the first bite of the forbidden fruit but Eve why because she wanted to be like God for some ladies that want to think like a man don't be deceived for all that lies ahead is call greed in the end only God will win.

At the whipping pole they use the cat-of-nine-tails and tore our Lord and savior back apart and for that reason we're blessed that our body will come together in the name of

Christ Jesus and receive the healing that our body need and required for the reason at the whipping pole Jesus make our healing successful and doable to he or she that believe and have no doubt.

Loved by God

There are two words to remember if you want to have peace with our God and they are as follow (love God) Two words from man that will please God they are (have faith) 3 words from God was enough to create the universe and they were (let there be) 4 words from God and they are as follow (you must live holy) Four words from our God would have been enough to create all mankind and they would be (let there be life) Just think 5 words from God have saved all mankind (the gift of my son) Now six words back to abab Father God from his son Christ Jesus they are (Now my father it is finished)

You know there aint know way you can fail when climbing to the peak of a mountain with Gods love and with God watching. A message to all Gods children when you have a mountain to climb and our Lords are there upon you know theres not one mountain that to high and if you look a little closer you will only see just a hill and then look even further down the way you will only see flat land why because God has already prepared and smooth out the way for your path.

There are some people doing enough to get into heaven and some people who are doing more and some people are doing much more for the glory and the kingdom of heaven and now there are some people that does a little wrong and know that it's wrong and will jeopardize going to hell and some that does much more wrong and there are people that does all the evil that they can to please Satan as they await their Journey to the pits of Hell could it be possible that we will get rewarded for the level of work that we did for the kingdom of heaven but in hell is sin just sin on the devil's in.

God is our Rock and salvation instead of picking up the Rock which is God's good word and placing it in to our heart some have the nerves to toss the word of God to the ground and then begin kicking it around therefore some have truly have missed out on the true love of God.

False politicians

There are lots of friendly politicians that lied their way into office and once they are there it's time for their true colors to come out why because they are not your true leader so then problems arise then it's time to pick a side and now they begin stepping on the back of the poor just to convince the other side.

Children like getting present for birthday and Christmas as they grow up and become adults hoping that they would rejoice and receive the most wonderful present of all and that is the persence of the most high God in our life.

The prayer Grace and Glory

Maybe you should not turn down the prayers of a unsaved person because one day the Lord made decided to open up the windows of Heaven and hear their prayer to say now that you have decided to seek my face you may now behold and receive my Glory and as well my grace that I have held back for you for such as a time as this that you shall stand fast and be unmovable for the kingdom of God (thank you God)

Who can say

Who can say in heaven that we may not have had a spiritual conversation with God before we was place in to our earthly body and put into our mother's womb something that we may not remember but it could have happened we may not remember but our God has not forgot

Hail and Hell

We know that God blowed into the nostrils of men and life began so inhale to acccept New Life and now through those same nostrils you must now exhald breathing out to sustain life as you keep our Gods name first as you continue on with your life by the love of God that you may Escape hell now look back over the two words that's differently spelled hail and hell where one is hot and not a very good place to stop

Don't drown for sin

If you would imagine people taking them problems to the cross and deposited them at the foot of our Christ and before Jesus could even close his eyes they were keeling down not praying but retrieving those very same sin and problems it's like when you pray and ask God to take your problems and throw them into the sea of forgetfulness and can you also imagine the people diving into that very same sea in even before there problems could even touch the bottom of the sea floor now can you picture those very same people whom knowing that they don't even know how to swim so they would eventually drown to death while trying to retrieve there sin that they have just laid down but not truly ready to release them out of their life so now they have accepted into their life a early death for the wickedness of their sin Amen

Not so good choice

Think about this why does some people knowingly or unknowingly allow otherr people the right to dictate where they will spend eternity when they should actually be bowing down on their knees and praying before our God instead your allowing some person that's in your life whom wont commit to you through marriage or who wont even truly help them to Carrie or even bear there burden but they do give them the right to madke a final decision for them that have you laying on a Unholy made-up be which will leave you right into the fiery pits of hell which is not where you want to reside or even lay there for one day so just think about laying there burning each and every moment about a choice that you could have made differently when it came to living and serving the lord

Bless it

Bless it thee that stand against sin and will fight for our God's right even until the very end because we know what awaits us he has said it through his words God have already worked all things out for his good and yours as well so hold on tight to your faith and never give up the fight because our God already have a way of making things workout right Amen

Good doctors

There are very many good doctors and then there are a few that only see dollars and not people's as there patients but with the mentality of the more patients I see the more dollars that comes to me there should be less thought on the money and more concentration on the reason for the place and position that our God have allowed for you to be.

Why lie about the truth

To all of the preachers that feels it's all right to tickle your congregation ears you best believe that Jehovah our God is not laughing in heaven so therefore you best believe you won't be laughing there either when it comes to receiving your reward in heaven so therefore it's now time for you to stop fabricaing the truth and allow God's real words to come through that it will illuminate our God's truth. Amen

Your miracle

People constantly ask our God for a miracle when God created you he also have place the miracle that you would desire on the inside of your body now you need to accept that gift which you already possess and thank God for it as you pull your miracle from that spiritual realm to the natural realm like saying you now have brought that miracle that God given you into the light so that all may believe

Holy dirt

Just think when God spit into the dirt in order to give the blind man sight now continue further back when God pick up dirt from the ground then he created man by blowing air into man nostrils then later on things began to turn bad but then God made them right again by the crucifixion of his son Christ Jesus we can now live holy for God and continue to do his Will to love one another as God loved his children in time things will go back to the way it was from dust we where made to dust we will return except our spirit and soul will live on until our God call us home Praise God

Just a dream

There was two warring gangs battling over destroyed real estate property that didn't belongs to either one of them but then they began fighting against each other then these large birds came into the picture and they did not discriminate or take a side they begin to destroy and eat both of the gangs that was warring with each other so in the end no one wins

Be anxious for nothing

We are just human and then the Bible said be anxious for nothing because that is just another form of nervous energy which is another word for anxiety and the only true way to get rid of that spirit is to call upon the blood of Jesus for that's stressful Spirit to leave you alone

Our God solid land

We walked this world on all types of terrain not really knowing where we may end up but for sure the lord always lead his children into the way of righteousness no matter how rocky things may get the Lord god of heaven will always lead his people through Terra firma so continue to march on and fight a good fight in Jesus name Amen.

The past

You can't ulter the pass but you can change the future. It's true we don't know all the bad and wrong that Satan has set up for our lfe but we can change them by accepting the plan that our God have set up for our life through God's son Christ Jesus

To Mom

To my mother from your son Tommie a word from God all the work that you have done for the kingdom of heaven has been received by God so now his words to you is that your work in words is not forgotten not for a day in hour or minute not even one second has been lost for our God kingdom 7

God's glory

Some people have been in church just about all of their lives a place of worship again I say will you now allow the church to do God's will but we know that in the end times x Jesus will return for his why is God's children so now is the time for you to let the church out of you so that the world might see the glory of God that lives inside of you after all you are the church

Students

Just thank we're students of the Holy Spirit that desire to dwell within us and to teach us the ways of our God we will never fully understand but we must start somewhere in order for us to start comprehend the truth that awaits our spirits it's all about the will and wanting to learn to accomplish this class in order to stay on the right Journey to God and to accomplish the guidance of the holy spirit that he have place in US to make the journey much more manageable

I suncerely feel that we should have a spiritual talk with God and ask him to remove the scales of doubt from our eyes that may see our true calling from Heaven in respond to the calling that he has placed in our life for his glory.

False seeker

For the hypocritical people that is walking our God world that is teaching themself how to lie to their self but one thing for sure you cannot lie to a righteous God there are some people that is seeking Our God face not out of love but the feat that the pandemic that is gripping this world and when the pandemic leave so will your need to seek our father god face so now to the ones of you whom now is call the great Pretender you may stop seeking our God face but there will become a time when you seek and cannot find a trace of our God face that you had betrayed back in the pastime

You can't take it with you

This is one thing you might have heard when you die you can't take it with you and that is ture to a certain point why because all of your good deeds has already went before you as Christians and as a sinner it's still the same but as a sinner some also may have lagged behind you and that is what's going to push your soul to hell

Not so good grief

God gave us the Earth and then he gave us life, as well free will then he even give us a part of himself as well then he turned around and gave us the life of his only son then in return for his goodness and mercy we turned around and gave God our rejection grief and unbelief and everything that was not Worthy to give a loving God that he did not deserve like refusing to show love for his son Christ Jesus so now in these last days is when we will have to make Amendment for the atonement for our sin and now it's time for our grief as well dishonor and pain to set in for our Sins. Given to his children's reluctantly and regretfully by a loving God Praise to our Lord

Jesus Paid the price

Jesus chose to have pay the price why because no one else qualified that mean we was lost as well full of sin so we was delinquent on paying the cost so Christ Jesus kindly stepped in and made the deal as he paid the price that no one else could have done so you now need to pass it on by picking up your cross because you sure know that everybody have a cross to bear so that our Lord don't have to continue and bearing the cross alone, so that we all can share in the kingdom of heaven when it comes to time to accept the immaculate place that we call our Heavenly home

The world transgressions

We give the praises to our Father God for allowing his son Christ Jesus to make Our apologies for our transgression against His holy name by being nailed to the cross. And while hanging from the cross during the darkest moment for a time Christ's spirit stepped down from the cross for a short time to pay a visit to the pits of hell where he's taking the keys from around the neck of Satan and also from death then Jesus return back to the cross where he reported back to our Father God that it is finished then as Jesus was descending back into heaven while passing up the Holy Spirit Jesus kindly place the keys around the neck of the Holy Spirit so now all that accept the Holy ghost becomes the holder of those very same keys in now have been drafted into the family of the Kingdom of Heaven and now Let the church say Amen

Grounded for life

Satan tries to throw up in front of God people's their pass meaning that he wants to try and hinder your future instead of looking back we should look forward fo the gift and plans that our God have for our life so don't be sidetracked or hindered about the lies that Satan have try to place in our life for after all he is the master of Illusionist and the Prince of Darkness which means that he could never really ever come Into The Marvelous Light so he have created his only dark light in lies and now have to stance back into the darkness of night like a wingless bird that will never ever take flight and that's is what we as Christians will call Satan for eternity which is the rest of his life the unflatable one (amen)

A dream of prevention

I believe before the Optical that appeared and my eye has happen my God has already given me the Cure due to the fact that I didn't pay attention I had to face the consequences that could have been avoided Sunday night I went to sleep and dream about my deceased brother and dad that they were in a swimming pool that had no water and it but they were holding up keys to me in their hands so I up that Monday morning and then that nigwokeht I dream that I was at some lady house that I didn't know then she began to walk through each and every room turning on every light in the house so I thought her to be strange so then we left her house and went over to my house again she started to walk through each and every room turn on each light so as she began to leave a little child appeared that was not there at first then the lady begain walked away saying and I will be back Thursday to pay you your money in my thought worth that she owed me no money that was Tuesday morning and then Tuesday night I begin to dream that the blood an one hand but was only boiling in just one finger that was making it way to the top of my finger in that was Wednesday morning and then through the day and then when night begin to occur I had the loudest ringing in my head I have ever had so I still went to sleep that night and for some reason the next day I decided to check my eyes and found out that I was losing sight in my left eye eventually I thought+ back on my first dream now I realize that the keys that my people was holding up to me were the one that I was to use to rebuke in bind the problem that was a about to take place with eyes really some dream should not be overlooked but taking as a warning gift for your well-being from our God

My dream

I just had a dream this night January 12, 2020 that I went to the restroom to wash my eyes in the name of the father the son and the Holy Spirit as I was geginning to watch them in the name of the Holy Ghost it was like something try to pull my hand away but it wasn't successful for I wash them anyway in the name of the Holy Spirit so that is when I got up and went to the restroom and did what I was instructed by the Holy Spirit and wash them in the name of the father in the son and the holy spirit then I began to feel God spirit move with and myself

Job opportunity

There are billions of people that is not working and say that they can't find a job and God Kingdom there are all types of wonderful search Opportunity for jobs like works of Miracles works of prophet sizing in the gift of healing ARe just a few of the jobs that can befill with full benefits at the end of Your retirement for example like free Heavenly care a lovely and holy Spirit-filled mansion and Golden Slippers Plus much more awaits you after completing the job that God has placed in your life for he is a wonderful employer will full in loving benefits for his children's (praise God).

Money is energy

When your lights goes out at yur home then you lose its energy through the house when you work out you also lose energy through your body, and then a little or not enough sleep can drain your energy also by being sick can take away your energy but to receive money can give you energy so to some people's money is energy but the real energy come from the blood of the Lamb. So now it's time to pour the full gospel in the only blood of Jesus up on yourself and order for the true energy to survive Amen

Pandemic War

In the last days there will be talk of wars and rumors of wars but now that this coronavirus pandemic has taken place The talk of wars and rumors of wars have now taken a back row seat now the talk is about finding a cure for the disease now Nations is no longer a guest Nation but now want to pull together for there survival wow looking for that cure to sustain life that just goes to show how fake this world really is why because when a cure is found Wars and rumors of wars will resume and Nations against Nations will find their way back to that place of hatred it sjust like saying that the disease was just a temporary setback now hatred can resume never having to go away again Elise not until the next pandemic shows its powerful hand of the return of our Lord and savior Christ Jesus and then these uncommon days would surely have to come to an abrupt end

New birth into the body of Christ

Just think before labor and birth a lady water breaks and then New Life Begin now think on the cross when a speared pierced Christ in the side in what was release was blood and in water that represent New birth into the body of Christ for the forgiveness of our sins that brought us back into the family of God and then what was said at the end was that (it is finished).

True faith

All true Faith lead to heaven and all lies will need a alibi which don't exist for you know that it's hard to keep a lie straight in your mind usually confusion come and not really abe to find a place to stay wow clogging up your mind as its Steal your soul and Spirited Away

Greed not need

There is something seriously wrong when a dictator uses chemicals against his very own people in the means of chemical warfare in other countries proceed comeing to there aid which is important that they do intervene so why in America doesn't the government come to the aid of their very own people or why do they allow the farmers to put chemicals into the food in meat of the American people that kills in Maine her people the chemicals like---n---nitroso-compounds-pesticide-steroids-in growth hormones to make the animals much bigger and larger so who's to say that when we cook the meats in food that the hormones doesn't continue to live on inside of the animals body that could also make us obese. And make us more open to all type of sickness illness and disease so you may say the government is for the people's not as much as they are for their own pockets greed superseded life when it comes to their own needs

26 letters in the alphabet

Our healing came through Christ Jesus At The Whipping Pole where 39 strikes to his body was received even for all of our future illness, sickness, and disease and by faith if you don't believe then those stripes was wrongly received and that I don't believe in food for thought There are 26 letters in the alphabet and every known illness sickness and disease can be spelled out through those letters that means the healing and cure that you desire was really spelled out through these very same letters at the whipping Pole and by the shedding of Christ Jesus blood our Lord and savior it did also spell out our cure for our souls salvation

The whipping Pole

At the whipping pole they use the cat-of-nine-tails and tore our Lord and savior back apart and for that reason we're blessed that our body will come together in the name of Christ Jesus and receive the healing that our body need and required for that reason at the whipping pole Jesus make our healing successful and doable to he or she that believe and have no doubt.

Bitter taste

To all women and men who want to play your mate for a sucker you can only play and lick on that sucker for so long and after that you know that your sucker is gone and you are now left with a unhappy home all because you play that so-called sucker wrong and you are now left with abitter taste in your mouth as well as alone

Just enough

There are some people doing enough to get into heaven and some people who are doing more some people are doing much more for the glory and the kingdom of heaven and now there are some people that does a little wrong and know that it's wrong and will jeopardize going to hell and some that does much more wrong and there are people that does all the evil that they can to please satan as they await their Journey to the pits of Hell could it be possible that we will get rewarded for the level of work that we have done for the kingdom of heaven but in hell is sin just sin on the devil's inn.

Heavenly Body

There was a time when the elderly paid us to lift boxes and some other heavy items and now that we have become elderly we also now pay the young people to perform some of the same chores that they paid us for an other words that is a never-ending cycle and will not stop until we receive our healthy bodies that we know will be presented to us.

The prayer Grace and Glory

Maybe you should not turn down the prayers of a unsaved person becaue one day the Lord may decide to open the windows of Heaven and hear that sinner prayer to say now that you have decided to seek my face you may now behold and receive my Glory as well as my grace that I have held back from you for such as a time as this that you shall stand fast and be unmovable for the kingdom of God (thank you God)

a person that desires to be a lost soul

Evil live in the sould of a unscrupulous person that refused to denounce evil and take into there life the will in the ways so therefore nothing good a wait the evil ones but a shell field with fire and brimstone that weights for them and the pits of hell Broad onto themselves for their disobedience to the words of God as well our Lord and to each other's therefore repent that you may come back into the grace of God

Satan very last fall

for Lucifer was addressed in heaven as the bright and Morning Star that must have slept with the cover of deception over his head that blinded his sight with in his mind so much that he thought that he could take over heaven and another blind moment is when he free Barabbas in order to crucify Christ instead again another dark moment for Satan Journey that cost him to make another Unholy decision one that he could not recall back but did bring again himself one more downfall now this will be considered his next to the very las fall as he attemt to Concord the land of Israel and now for his very last fall he will be tossed down into the pits of hell where he will make his last call as well his very final fall amen

Bad Company

It's bad when they say that misery love company why because as time go on things can get even worse if that miserable person still can't find a suitable companion to keep their Disturbed mind occupied at least not one for a long period of time they're Disturbed Souls began to fight against their god-given spirit and then torment takes hold not willing to let go now Satan began to place his feet up on their neck an ungodly thoughts within there troubled mind and now they are much more confused now then ever before but you know that your love continues on even does that the person that has no love for you at least none that you can see but does show a large amount of animosity and hate for you God says love your neighbors which is your rebellious children also, ask yourself but the Ludacris part about it is that you love them more then they love themselves for all is not lost when you seek the one true God and learn to rebuke the thoughts of Satan

Your congregation

A word to some pastors and Revelations also you know whom this speak to but our God knew it first about how you sometimes use reverse psychology on your congregation I would not say that you are lying but just another way of letting your congregation know the needs of the church for it does take money to advance the kingdom of heaven and God has more than enough to meet his need to ask for much more it could be considered as greed

The crucifixion

Thanks to Abba Father God Son Christ Jesus for allowing himself to be nailed to the cross and thanks also to the one that lifted and raised the cross from the ground that draw all Mankind back into the grace of God and that was done for everyone that wants to accept Jesus crucifixion unto themselves as we kneel at the foot of the cross

Truetide

Could there be a Biblical cord thats Tided to God's children from Heaven to Earth that heightened in increase faith that cannot be seen by The natural human eyes and through thatcord we communicate through the Holy Spirit to our Heavenly Father and doing that time Satan does his best to manipulate as well to interrupt that line it may seem to have happen for a short time but then it's reconnected as though it has never been broken and our God spiritual eyes that's why we live for God and do all that is righteous and spoiling the plots that Satan has already plotted against mankind in other words against all our Gods children.

Does tomorrow exist

Have you ever taken the time to see how useless that tomorrow is why because for the simple fact that tomorrow isn't promised to any one man or woman so be wise and use the gifts in ths moment of time that our God have blessed you with for this world is not our home, but just abab father way of a loan and the time given to our God children's is not there own but to be shared with others on our God given journey to heaven which is our Heavenly eternal real home so let's not reflect on tomorrow for we no not what tomorrow brings for tomorrow will take care of itself. Amen

Peoples to be accepted

Do you believe the Bible when it says pray for the head of your leadership, which now seems to be president-elect Vice President Biden and vice president-elect Harris as President and Vice President for we know many Christians wanted to see a Trump and Pence re-election it was not meant to be successful but all things work out for the good of our God so therefore it must have been Gods will and not he will of man therefore that's why those two people prevail, for you should know that God makes no mistakes so therefor elect Biden and Harris must hae been placed there for such a time of as now for we know that the end time prophecies are being fulfiled and that everyone has a part in the scene, so why be shocked at the outcome for we know to our God that there's no new news because everything under the Sun has already been done so now it's time for all of us to except the outcome but there will always be some hypocritical people whom don't want to see things done GODs way for it will be our saviors ways and for all of you people that are embracing a Stony heart it's time to let go so that you may embrace your part and continue our Gods will Amen

Some may remember

Some may remember when the president to be Joe Biden said to the Speaker of the House Nancy Pelosi that my house is your house not knowing that his house would be a cabinet room inside the White House an then he would be placed second incommand. And then vice-president Kamala Harris will be third in command. So the truth head leader of the White House would be Nancy so don't be surprised if there would be a cat fight inside the White House because vice President Harris might not take it so lightly being demoted to thirst in command, so now the cats fight in the White House will begin one will lose the other one will win.

Defender

Defend it Our Father God who sits on his heavenly throne as the true judge of all mankind with the gavel of righteousness within his right hand for only the truth will be reveal And all other untruth will be denied so now it is time for your Defender to plead your case

That is where Christ Jesus come in with his Saving Grace to plead to the father on your behalf for your misdeed with no intent for you to deceive so now you should thank the Lord for pleading your case and thank Our god for showing you his love is Saving Grace

Heavenly plan

How can we accept the keys to the Kingdom of Heaven when there are so many of us still refusing to recognize what our Christ did for us on the cross. We should be filled with more incredible praising and worshipping through Christ Jesus that our Father God would call us Worthy of his Amazing Grace, now that we have been redemmed from the sin of Eve and Adam once again we are his children's and now can receive the keys to God kingdom of heaven for we know that no man can enter heaven without Takeing

Christ Jesus as their lord and savior so you should forfeit you're sin and accept Jesus as the son of man then our father God will include you as part of his heavenly family again for we should all acknowledge that there's truly only one way end amen,

A pace of mine

I got to hold a piece of Sanity in my head whom think on the behalf of others as there mind are running and thanking scare for you know that our God has never gave us the spirit of confusion but if you have it that means that you allow Satan to place it there in order to remove it all you need is a Heavenly prayer

No feeling

When you allow people to walk over you some family members are just as bad so you call yourself not wanting to hurt their feelings so you bite your tongue knowing that they don't care so when you bite down on your tongue you're the only one that feels the pain why because others just don't care

Deceitfulness

Food For Thought could it be that this pandemic actually did not start in China But in Africa where it could have been placed there by a certain group of mankind to destroy a race of peoples in now this pandemic has came home to roost or to surround its creator in all of mankind covering the whole world and all its peoples for the sin of a few that have had deceitfulness in their minds for a cetain race of god children And now could it be that God have allowed this pandemic to visit all mankind for a season again for the sin of a few sometimes a lot have to pay the price not that it be God's will but for man devious ways

??? Which one

I think Abba Father God for his son Christ Jesus which is the word in the Holy Spirit which teaches the word that reflex the love and word of God by receiving Jesus whom is the word that brings us back into the Covenant Our Father God.

Our god of hosts gives his invitation through the word which is his son Christ Jesus for we know that no man can enter the kingdom without going through his holy word Christ

Jesus which can be seen and learnt through the free gift of the Holy Spirit so now will be a good time to open up your heart to receive the goodness of our God Words which is his son Christ Jesus

We work on our Earth job for wages and should get paid for the work accordingly now think about your soul and how it will be paid for your Heavenly work for you nothat the wages of sin is death so we should be putting our spirit and will together for God good while making disciple for the kingdom of heaven as we glorify Our Father which is in heaven whom hold the keys of eternal life in the palm of his hand therefore you should think before you decide to sin so that you may make eternal life your choice before the very end.

In certain places

God put people in certain places but not known to them so that they may watch over us in not known to us he put ourself in certain places to watch over others but in the end it's God whom watches over us all

In the end time

Our body returns back to the Earth when we are deceased as Christians our soul is now set free and now once again our spirit Rejoice as it reconnect back to abab father god

Jesus The Rock an...

People said you gotta hit rock bottom if you have any types of addiction in your life if you want to ride to the top. First of all you need to stop giving Satan the free rein to run through your mind. While at the bottom now you need to praise that rock and rebuke any type of addition that had you bound now please them on the ground then covered them back with The Rock you can stand upon the rock because it truly represent our Lord and savior. Now say to The Rock what I've buried will never come back to the top praise God.

They have denied Jesus

They have removed Jesus from the courthouse and they have also remove him from the schools and now it can be said that you have denied Jesus before man now Jesus will also deny you before his father now whom have the most to lose

Being for real

As a female role model for your god-given Earthly daughter and also as the male role model for your god-given Earthly son but just maybe in the beginning you didn't know how to relate to things that was happening in your life as well your child's life. So that stress was too great for you to handle. So then you decided to depart from the scene. As time went by our God was graceful enough and giving you a second chance for you to be graceful but instead some parents chose not the correct path when coming back into their childrens life. By taking there kindness for weakness and still some parents are still making poor decisions it was not wrong that our Lord allowed you a second chance but that you refused to make good with that chance. So now all that can be said is may Our God bless you but not your deceitful ways

A Lost calling

Do you remember back in the old days when there was a few people in the Upper Room moving around like they was intoxicated but yet still they had not taken one drop of alcohol. Now why today does it seemed like these very special peoples are so very hard to locate, most likely because we do not seek the Holy Spirit as we should and thats very unfortunately because in these time as well days when we should be pulling God closer instead of casting our Lord Holy Spirit further away

Theses are just short saying

Those mountain won't move by themself but they will be move with our God's help,

The only hope for mankind is when they allow Jesus to infiltrate their very sinnful heart and mind

I thank God for the skills that he placed in these very special surgeon hands of the doctors, and to Christ Jesus for taking into his very special hands the nails of faith and miracle healing,

(Jesus the great physician spiritually and physicans healer)

We know that the air can't be seen but can be felt on our skin caused by the blowing of the Wind on our skin felt but not seen So therefore the miracle of faith also

Justice to be or not to be

Food for thought just think about it that the only time that Lady Justice put on and wear her mask is when there's a set time for a rich Elite person that needs to be put on trial then down Comes the Mask so that all of the evidence will not be seen so it won't be justified and counted against them so now it's time for the less fortunate one to come to trial then the mask comes off then Lady Justice will see things as she wish therefore the sentence that should have been passed down on the rich seems like it's divided between the less fortunate one which mean Justice is not necessarily fair or even equal but that it the way that lady Justice see things but only when I'll our Lord and savior Jesus Christ returns for his children will true Justice be Prevail in handed out to Us all equally praise be to God

Pure of heart

God say we must be pure in heart after all we are human and spiritual beings. Children of the Most High God at the same time Satan fights aganst our heart. As he tries to place uncleaniness in our souls as well as throughout our lives. But thanks to Our Father God it won't be so.

For two trees

Words for thought out of the two sacred trees that was placed and the midst of the garden of Eden. That the tree of life was place there for such as a time that we are facing now. for God knew that man would sin and come short of God glory so could the Tree of Life represent the sacrificial cross that our Lord Jesus Christ would be crucified upon for the Redemption of the Sins of all mankind to retrieve all of God's children back unto the glory of God. And now for the touching in the eating from the tree of knowledge of Good and Evil for God knew that his children would not fully understand or comprehend the true meaning from the tree that represented the knowledge of Good and Evil. But they were told if they would eat from this tree that they will surely die and then their Disobedience set in then separation from Abba Father God did beginners.

Slippery Fox

You may help someone get back on their feet and then you even bless them with some food to eat then you turn your back and they still a second meal. so before you considered on getting some rest you should make sure that slippery Fox thing is address (meaning to be taken care of) because if you turn your back and that problem is not solved you best believe that slippery Fox will return in try to take it all away and that would be fine for the food that he is confiscating represent the words of God So let him continue to feed for the food that he's eating with Surely fulfill his in our God's need

Selfishness for some is a way

Some people go to life only doing what they can do for themselves and not someone else not realizing that only what we accomplished for God here on Earth will be justified and anything else will be denied

Distance

six feet is the safe distance for you and your neighbors wellbeing for life and another six feet is used when someone die and that is the distance for death and burial and now the third of three six is the mark of the beast which you don't want to receive but truly distance yourself from so that, you will become close with no distance between you and our Father God.

The church

When Jesus comes back for the church during the rapture he is not coming back for a building because we know that he have already established a mansion in heaven for his children so we should rejoice and receive God's return as the children of God

The box

God want us to step outside the box which represents the world which is the garden to make saints out of the sinners by digging out the bad that represent chain that is trying to choke out the words of God and we know that not going to be successful because our God words will always prevail

Legalize marijuana

Now that they have legalized marijuana in their own ways what makes you think that they won't do the same with crack cocaine all for the Love of money and that will be the next cure for those who don't have the faith of Jesus Christ as their cure in their life

Don't drown for sin

If you would imagine people taking their problems to the cross and deposited them at the foot of our Christ and before Jesus could even close his eyes they were kneeling down not praying but retrieving those very same sin and problems it's like when you pray and ask God to take your problems and throw them into the sea of forgetfulness and can you also imagine the people diving into that very same sea in even before there problems could even touch the bottom of the seafloor now can you picture those very same people whom knowing that they don't even know how to swim so they would eventually drown to death while trying to retrieve there sin that they have just laid down but not truly ready to release them out of their life so now they have accepted into their life a early death for the wickedness of their sin Amen

When God speaks

When God spoke this world into existence then he said that it is good, later he created man and said it is good so we now think that man can destroy something that God said that it is good God made all preparation for all of his creations so the world has a way of sustaining its boundaries what you really need to be concentrating on is the need to bring the spirit of God back into a Lost world

The Sabbath

The Bible say on the Sabbath day you should rest does that mean on Good Friday the six day after taking Christ down from the cross after Jesus crucifixion the showing of his love for all Mankind the LED to the Lord Sabbath day and Jesus time of rest that then they place Jesus and the borrowed tomb, and on the third day our Lord did arise with all power in the palm of his hand given to CHRIST by abab father god for all whom believe

Rebuking mind

Sometimes death try to misuse its power by trying to take a person before their time that's when you have to rebuke the powers of death by bleeding the blood of Jesus after all our Lord Jesus Christ did defeat Hell Death and the name Satan and death at the cross on our behalf so therfore if its not your time you can rebuke and hang up that line on death call for father God has the correct time as well the calling back of our spiritual life in the end time, (praised be to our God)

Lost thought

··

You can laugh at the truth because you know what you're laughing about, but you can't laugh at a lie why because your mind may Have already forgot what you would have Been laughing about in other words a lie that your mind doesn't remember any way Amen

Already owned by God

··

Words for thought when people pay their tithes giving God the 10% that already belongs to him and then they turn right around and look for a 30-60-100 fold blessng forgiving God the 10% that already belongs to him do you feel that it's fair just think if someone owe you let's say $10 would you think that they are blessing you by paying your $10 back or are they just giving you what is yours already that is how you should see the 10% already as Gods funds now you ought all the think and know that your real blessing will come by you giving your offering in donations to the widows and orphans just as our God have suggested alone with a prayer for Thanksgiving addressed to abab Father God whom sit on his heavenly throne awaiting for you to ask then you will receive your blessings Amen

Saving Grace

If you speak it you may forget it but if you write it down then one day you might regret it

(Not lost but reconnected)

As a Christian to be absent from this world is to be reconciled with God in the Heavenly Realm (Amen)

(A job well done)

Being To be a Christian when you leave this earth there should be no remorse for God's angels in heaven are truly rejoicing for here on Earth you have done your work now it's time for you to return home so that you Will receive your reward

(Our God Delight)

(all Praise be to our God)

(out of our hand)

When things may seem bad write it down and place it in God's hand and have no doubt for our God will surely work things out

A divided world

for we know that people divided against each other will surely collapse in other words they cannot stand or A House Divided will quickly fall or a nation divided will war against itself therefore if a world is divided it will eventually come to an end. Why because there's no real love to hold it together so now stupidity comes along with sin an some Revenge giving Satan a reason to laugh while the world implode from within as satan put his plan into motion while shifting forward into gear for those whom chooses not to repent hell draws near and a eternal damnation that surely will never disappear

A Vanishing panademic

We know that the spirit of this pandemic have no fear it dosen't discriminate and will take you away from this world at the same time we know that this pandemicis is no match for our Lord Christ Jesus so therefore we should seek our

Jesus face so that our God face will appear and remove this worldwide pandemic away from here amen.

Our God transportation

For we know ask Christians when it's time for us to leave this world then the ship of Zion will appear therefore we know that our God is near to take his child away from here with no stop in between then there. We shell behold a beatiful heaven seen praise be to God

Just one day

Words for thought was we really meant to be born and live here on Earth for just one day before we sin in the garden of Eden against our Holy Father then doing that particular time Satan appeared into the picture where he threatened our peace and also the happiness of the garden that God had called our home in for that interruption that Satan had cost in the garden he will have to pay for one day by being Chained and cast into the Lake of Fire. Now lets think back on Adam who lived to the rightful age of 930 just think 70 more years he would have been 1,000 years of age could that mean that the last 70 years would be the remainder of the time that Adam would have received for the rest of his life but due to sin in the garden, life was cut short can you imagine that if there was no sin in the garden that you could have lived to be 1,000 years of age because to our Lord one day is as a thousand years, that may have been our lifespan if it wasn't forsinning in the garden instead of the 70 years that was left on Adams life

The Great I Am

Moses asked God his name and the words that was spoken to Moses were that my name is I am that means your everything from the shoes that your feet walk in the body that you process an every breath that leaves your body I am a doctor also the Messiah as well your host in the house that you also live in therefore I am your everything but most of all I'm your lord and savior

False prophet or Antichrist

I had a dream about Reverend parsley preaching at his church and when the sermon was finished he just fell backwards on the pulpit and began to laugh hysterically and saying I just got over on the congregation but the more I look at it clearly it was then revealed to me through the revelation of the Holy Spirit that shows me that it was not the Reverend parsley but President Donald Trump on the rebel Pulpit looking to deceive the congregation and as well the entire world and that he as president could possibly be the false prophet or the Antichrist so now that the corona have appeared so close to election time now Trump want to be the savior of Americans by passing out stimulus money over the USA money that represent the word seeds So now that he have done so what would Now be his reward or his Harvest, possibly whateer he desire most likey another turn in the white house as your president So now that he may have paid his way back into the White House he May have one more stay all because he gave you back the money that belongs to you anyway, you remember that saying that nothing is free for it was your hard-earned money that you have worked for that you have possibly received from the false prophet or the Antichrist that would never have done you a good deed. Now go back to the beginning of the dream all he wanted to do was to deceive by trying to make this World Harvest fall to it's knees-but thank God You know the devil will never succeed (praise go to our god Yahweh)

It doesn't all add up

Be fruitful and multiply and how do we multiply when millions of God's babies have being aborted by man, and as the time of old Babylon which exists right now today that men are still lovers of each others and some women's only bond with other women so therefore Some peoples are still not taking Gods word to heart, so you should now think about all of the Generations of babies that have been aborted and taken out of Gods will that abab father god had for this world that we shall be fruitful and multiply

a person that desires to be a lost soul

Evil live in the soul of a unscrupulous person that refused to denounce evil and take into there life the will in the ways of our Lord Christ Jesus so therefore nothing good a wait the evil ones but a shell field with fire and brinstone that weights for them and the pits of hell bought on themselves for their disobedience to the words of God as well as our Lord to each other therefore repent that you may come back into the grace of God

Jesus Brides

Some People have just about been in church all of their life or the place that they meet is a place of worship again I say will you now allow the church to do Gods will for we know that in the end time: Jesus will return for his bride which is God Church so now is the time for you to let the church out of you so that the world may see the glory of God that lives inside of you.

Trumpcare

Could it be that they will overturn Roe versus Wade which is a very good thing so that they will stop killing God's offspring and could it also be that they may overturn Obamacare that could harm the poor, sick, and the elderly and take away their health care for this will be just another form of a way to demolish the poor, sick, and elderly again just another form of Roe versus Wade to kill the government way that now can be called the Trump care or the Trump I don't care. (or would it be either if he don't win)

Not our battle

When Satan tries to inflict trouble your way the best thing to do is drop on your knees and pray while directing the problems and the troubles that Satan had for you, Our God way for we know that the battle is not ours but the Lords and for the one whom started the War we battle against him no more for the victory goes to our Lord (Amen to the glory of God)

Negativity

It's not property that kills but leak of knowledge and unsaved people that won't get together with God's children in defeat that negativity should have never exist in God's world because at the cross Jesus conquered it all

Bad money

Peoples say that money is the root of all evil. Have you ever heard money speak, saying that I'm going to think for myself and also spend myself or how about I think God for creating me but I decide not to pay God the 10% creation fee which is my tithe. Or money say I think I'm going to buy me a gun, to protect my wealth, or visit the casino and gamble Myself

Away and as money I Am My Own Boss. So I don't wish to help Gods needy ones, only myself, so just think money is not the root of all evil but in the wrong hand it's no help, because selfish peoples are only out to help themselves

Satan very last fall

for Lucifer was addressed in heaven as the bright and Morning Star that must have slept with the cover of deception over is head that blinded his sight with in his mind so much that he thought that he could take over heaven another blind moment is when he free Barabbas in order to crucify Christ instead again another dark moment for Satan Journey that cost him to make another Unholy decision one that he could not recall back but did bring again himself one more downfall now this will be considered his next to very last fall as he attempt to Concord the land of Israel and now for his very last fall he will be cast down into the pits of hell where he will make his last call as well his very final fall Amen

Thanksgiving

People have really failed to know the true meaning of Thanksgiving so many of us think that it's on one day in the month of November. Now let the truth be told each and every day that God give you is his way of showing you his love and grace in Thanksgiving so therefore we should be giving more thanks and praise to God for each day is a moment that you should be thankful for Amen

More valuable with time in age

When people say I'm just old I beg the difference you are not old but you are older money does age and gets old with time and so much more valuable as well as a fine wine that gets better with time so the more we age the more we are filled with wisdom and knowledge, that could be a blessing to others so you should be wearing your age as a badge of honor for each passing day is a blessing

When the earth speaks to God

Does the groundgroaning and if man doesn't praise our God will the rock shout out and worship His holy name after all God did remove dust from the ground to create Life For All Mankind so why can't the groundgroaning all We Are All Made of the same substance so why can't this Earth feel remorse and Show it by groaningout for the disrespect that mankind have shown to our Heavenly Father

(Think about it)

So just think if the groundgroaning out end was in pain due to man neglect it didn't open up to receive our seed offering then there would be no Harvest no due to the Lords love but that disrespect of all mankind (Amen)

Lost but still can be gained

for this pandemic doesn't necessarily have to come from God why? because Satan is known as the prince of the air and does have the freedom to glide on the air just as the pandemic does after all he is the one prince of the air that can spread the deadly disease, but our God always have a plan of protection for his children in one way or another and his name is Jesus and most likely in times like these which feels like Solomon and Gomorrah where sin was so great that the Lord our Father God had decided to remove His Hedge of protection and now could it be that God have did the very same thing to this sinful world of peoples that refuses to seek our God face and wake up and so now unmercyness have been placed in front of us almost like decree that Gods children that's filled with love grace and mercy have almost lost a holy friend but, do to Gods love we know that Redemptions, it's always at hand so be blessed and turn from your sinful ways so that our God will place his hedge of protection back over our world again (Amen)

Bad fruit

Just think if you had the True faith of a mustard seed and believe as Jesus did like when he spoke to the fig tree and cursed it now just think if you would speak to cancer diabetes or any other type of heart defect as though you was talking to the Fig Tree but instsead use whatever type of illness or sickness that's troubling you in its place and watch it withered away for it has no place to survive and will not be able to catch roots, therefore it would not be able to hold on to the life that's in our bodies but will have to die out as the Fig Tree did when our Lord Jesus Christ placed a curse up on the figs, you must do the same thing to your illness and accept the fact that you no longer sick praise God

We are Spirit, soul and body so Christians must think it's alright to drink alcohol because Jesus turned waterr into wine we must remember he didn't use those certain spirit ingredients to make it come alive but just love not stuff like yeast, sugar, and starch so buy man use what he used today now the spirit have come to life so when you drank that spirit of alcohol you only putting one spirit against the spirit that's already in your body and now they begin to fight to try and do what's wrong. And not right

Snake tiak

Food for thought: Just think when Eve was having a conversation with the snake he was telling her everything she wanted to hear and then see begin to hear what she wanted to hear from the mouth of Satan those words was spoken like Venom which in true form is another word for poison that Eve took into her body.

Mismanagement

Some people's can't manage their money correctly so in other words than means there money have takeing on authorization over them and now manage those people so now what we will soon see is call mismanagement because our money have takening on legs and have quickly ran out of your pocket and out from your possession. It's all right to use your money but another thing when you start allowing your money to use you

(just about)

It's not just about life and death (thank) But about life and faith through Christ Jesus now build your belief and watch your faith grow. Praise God

(your mind and heart)

Something maybe going on or happening in your mind that you can most likely handle or Define but if it breach your heart it just might be enough to pull you a part and vice a versa so don't allow satan thoughts to accumulate in your're mind that he may want to attack your eart at a later time so rebuke the thought in allow Jesus to make his home within your mind as well your heart. (Amen)

Insignificant

The devil is insignificant and that is why he tries to pick a fight with our God's children thinking that he can make them feel the same but it's not going to happen why because we are fighting him with the right ammunition which is the blood of the Lamb of God the more we bleed the blood the more he retreat so we should keep on stomping ours feet why becaue the devil is underneath and has already been declared defeated

Confused Spirit

to all of you who think that it's all right to attach yourself to the same gender like saying at the time of your birth you have changed your mine as well our God's mine for our God makes no mistakes about his creation just as he put Adam and Eve in the garden and not Mike and Ike so what needs to be done that you much become spiritually strong in our God but if not the devil will manipulate your mind and confuse your spirit

Bail out to

There's are some good in the bail out and bad also that weighs heavily on some people's (the bad) when you bail out the big company the stockholderrs get to keep there money in their pocket and then begin also to put your money in their pockets also the only decent thing about it that some Americans get to keep their job as they continue making a living for their family in at the same time the fat cat pockets continue to grow with a overflow of taxpayers dollars

Man very first

Just think where men first learn how to run from God and why. Just because of one bite from the forbidden fruit out of the garden of Eden where things really began to make a change because of submitting to the deceitful voice of Satan they also have learned how to try and hide to no reveal so now that they have realized And found out that there isn't no such place too hide not even in their mind for the sinners have now come together and now have allowed sin in which is willing to lead their way into a unholy place after judgement day has taken its place there will be so many peoples lost in sin but by choosing Christ Jesus for our savior we all can make amends before our life come to the end by claiming Gods son becaue there isn't anywhere else left for you to run

The garden

There was a tree place in the middle of a place called The Garden of Eden that tree is known as the tree of eternal life and then later there was one place on Mount Calvary for the one that was sinned against in the first place and Eden, the tree that was placed on Mount Calvary had someone very special nailed on it in order to make right for what was done wrong to the first one Christ Jesus gave his life that we may join back with our Father God that we may have eternal life something that was stolen from us out of the garden of Eden in the first place

Spanked

Love from our parents father God when we allow ourself to sin and do wrong again God we are chastise just saying being spanked by our heavenly Father so now as earthly parents do you not spank or chastise your earthly children for doing wrong but in the end someone will have to pay for our child sins so as the parent I would think that there sins would be charge to there earthly parent for not chastising or sanking your child here on Earth you have spared the rod and now have spoiled God's children here on Earth for they are known to us as our future generations parent's before friend if not there could be another Lost generation in the end.

Stolen 10%

to all whom steal from God that very first 10% and place it in their wallet you should know that in your pocket lies a very large and hungry hole that means the 10% seed that was stolen from God will fall to the ground and bear no good fruit you should also know that the same 90% that God has given you is also going into that very same pocket so now you have lost the whole hundred percent which 10% really never belongs to you in the first place

A talk with God

Maybe we should have a spiritual talk with God and ask him to remove the scales of doubt from our eyes that we may see our true calling for the kingdom of heaven and response to the True calling that he have already place and I'll life already to sufficiently and glorify the kingdom of our God from heaven

Some people's attitude

Some people have more attitude than they have gratitude when it comes to doing the will of God so you should lose the attitude and pray to our God that he gives you more gratitude when it comes to working for the kingdom of heaven

Some people are trying to be really slick for their own good not realizing that the person that they're really hurting is themselves because there are some people that wants to help them at time but it does no good and sometimes you just got to allow them to slip and slide on their own slickness that they may see the errors of their on devilish ways anorder for them to see our God light

Jesus Paid the price

Jesus chose to have pay the price why because no one else qualified that mean we was lost as well full of sin so we was delinquent on paying the cost so Christ Jesus kindly stepped in and made the deal as he paid the price that no one else could have done so you now need to pass it on by picking up your cross because you kow everybody have a cross to bear so that our Lord don't have to continue and bearing the cross alone, so that we all can share in the kingdom of heaven when it comes to time to accept the immaculate place that we call our Heavenly home

Overtime

food for thought have you ever taken the time and turn around and look back at the mountain that Jesus have just carried you over praising and thanking him for a successful trip that would not have been possible without his love on the journey that Jesus have carried us through for we know not the danger that we was surrounded by as we was being carried across the mountain and through the valley that should be enough to thank God for his present

Words for thought

Words for thought was it about the tree of Life yes it was end at the same time so much more God wanted to see if his children had the love and ability to obey his every word and not to show contempt to God by their disobedience but by doing so that's had led us into the wrong direction that the Lord has not set up for our life so it's now time for us to make right for what we had done wrong to a just and righteous God now all have been made right at the cross by thinking our God that all is not lost.

Signs in numbers

We know that signs and numbers have some types of biblical meaning like the number three is for the Trinity and 7 for the love of God now lets jump to 20/20 you know and eyes terms that it's like saying that you have almost perfect vision just think could this be the year that I'll God would remove the scales from his children spiritual eyes that they will see and work to uplift the kingdom of our Father God and squash The works of Satan

Wanting to steal your joy

For all of the peoples that's within the body of Christ that is in the hospital May our God's healing power enter into your room and take away what type of illness that want to steal your joy we need to thank strong and hold on to our God's faith as he carried us alone

Proper lies

yes God gave his prechers the ability to prophesize and then there are others that have the ability to tell proper lie those are the one that are trying to recoup their reward here on Earth by being disobedient to the true calling that God has placed on their lives and not on their lies

Not ordinary time.

Why some people think that we are living in ordinary time but as you look around and you will see that these are unordinary times and it is at this very moment that we should be seeking God's face for these extradordinary time we should be praying to our god that we be able to endure whatever Satan decide to throw our way we will pitch it back into the pits of hell

Satanic lies

What we know as Christians that schizophrenia is a spirit placed in the mind of God's children by Satan Just to try and confuse their spirits as well the calling that God has placed for there lifes therefore you should pray against that spirit in other words rebuke it in the name of Christ Jesus as well the blood soat Spirit will be forced to scatter from you then enter back into the pits of hell from which it came

Unnecessary feeling

What do you think about a person that constantly drop food on the front of his shirt or a lady that drops food on her dress you may come to several conclusion one is that they are just messy eaters or clumsy it could be that they just don't like eating alone so they feed their clothes that May means there are two lonely people that May need to get together in ordered that they may not allow their clothes to continuously get overweighted with food that their stomach should be enjoying get the point

Your faith

People pray to God and say Lord give me more Faith when its already been done as the Lord have said all you need is the faith of a mustard seed so what your prayer should truly be is Lord help my spirit to soar that my faith will increase as well my doubt decrease while we advnce forward giving your people's the good news of your soon return so while it's happening they won't have one eye open the other closed as you come back to receive your bride unto yourself Amen

Three crosses make one

Looking Through The Eyes of a unsaved soul there would be three crosses that their eyes would be hold that is because of the illusion that's playing tricks with their unbelief as well their unclean soul but when the spirit is purified as well our soul then the truth will be scene in toad because only one cross will your eyes behold why because our God has now intervene and now the one cross that you will see only have one entity Christ Jesus that's nailed on the cross that have delivered and save us all because the three crosses that you are looking at really represent just one crossed that have now pleased our God and now have clean our unworthy soul from the pits of hell a place that was not ever built for our God children's but for those one's who end up there they are only trespassing and also intruding on the house that our God has created for Satan and his followers

A constantly Running mind

Have you ever taking the time and thought about your mind and body how the mind constantly runs now think back about your body and how it ageist and break down through over working it or undere exercising the body knowing that it would never ever catch up to your mind at least not in this lifetime

The Peak

You know that there aint know way you can fail when climbing to the peak of a mountain with Gods love and with God watching over you: A message to all Gods cildren when you have a mountain to climb and our Lords spirit is there accompany you know theres not one mountain that to high and if you look a little closer you will only see just a hill and then look even further down the way you will only see flat land why because God has already prepared and smooth out the way for your Journey so praise God and begin you're holy trip

Gods love

God love us from the beginning of time and then our sins set in, instead of showing us his wraft God showed his children more love by allowing his son Jesus Christ to take our sins to the tree of Life to make amends but still we sin it will eventually have to make a abrupt end then our sins will come to a end.

The crucifixion

Thanks to Abba Father God Son Christ Jesus for allowing himself to be nail to the cross and thanks also to the one that lifted and raised the cross from the ground that draw all Mankind's back into the grace of God and that was done for everyone that wants to accept Jesus crucifixion unto themselves as we kneel at the foot of the cross

Your congregation

A word to some pastors and Revelations also you know whom this speak to but our God knew it first about how you sometimes use reverse psychology on your congregation I would not say that you are lying but just another way of letting yur congregation know the needs of the church for it does take money to advance the kingdom of heaven and our God have more then enough to meet his need ask for to much more it could be considered as greed

Bad Company

It's bad when they say that misery love company why because as time go on things can get even worse if that miserable person still can't find a suitable companion to keep their Disturbed mind occupied at least not one for a long period of time they're Disturbed Souls began to fight against their god-given spirit and then torment takes hold not willing to let go now Satan began to place his feet up on their neck an ungodly thoughts within there troubled mind and now they are much more confused now then ever before but you know that your love continues on even does that the person that has no love for you at least none that you can see but does show a large amount of animosity and hate for you God says love your neighbors which is your rebellious children also, ask yourself but the Ludacris part about it is that you love them more then they love themselves for all is not lost when you seek the one true God and learn to rebuke the thoughts of Satan

Moses ask God whom shall I say sent me and the words that was spoken to Moses was that my name is I am that I am meaning your everything from the shoes that your feet walk in the body that you process an every breath that leaves your body I am your doctor also the Messiah as well your host in the house that you also live in therefore I am your everything but most of all I am your lord and savior

When God removes...

Just think America have almost tried to drive the glory of God away from our nation thank back doing September 11, 2001 when God has taken his eyes off of America and now 2020 God have taken his eye off of America again why for the simple fact that America has once again taken there eyes off of God, now therefore non-believers now ask does God still love America yes even for the simple fact that you have turn your head and lost your site faith and believe doesn't mean that he don't but we really do need to return and seek his face that we may once again be brought back into Our Father God's grace